Alan Titchmarsh's Gardening Guides

CONT
GARDENING

HAMLYN

London · New York · Sydney · Toronto

Portable planters

Time was when anyone with only a backyard or doorstep to their name would have shrugged sadly at the mention of gardening. But today there's plenty of opportunity for decorating your doorstep or perking up your patio with a bevy of flower-filled pots and tubs, urns and troughs.

Don't convince yourself that pots are simply for summer. Filled with the right plants they can brighten your life during any month of the year, and their greatest advantage is their portability; when you tire of the scheme the pots can be re-arranged and replanted for a fresh effect.

So whether your garden is one of those concrete yards, endearingly referred to by estate agents as a town garden; whether it's no more than the balcony of a flat, a city rooftop, a couple of square metres (or yards) of concrete that you optimistically call a patio, or even a humble windowsill, start thinking about cheering it up with plants in pots. Whatever the time of year, now's the time to start.

A window box and one or two tubs thoughtfully planted can enliven the tiniest back yard. Evergreen shrubs and herbs are attractive and useful during most of the year

The basics

It really doesn't matter what container you use to hold your plants, provided it passes the following tests. It should be:

- Good looking yet not more showy than the plants
- Well drained (check for holes in the base)
- Capable of holding sufficient compost
- Positioned in good light
- Capable of retaining moisture
- Stable

It's always best to avoid brilliantly coloured containers – the flowers and foliage are supposed to be cheering you up, not the pots. If the pot is brightly painted the brilliance of the flowers will seem as nothing, which is why muted terracotta pots have been used with success for so long.

Very small pots can be a pain in the neck, for they'll dry out at the drop of a sun-hat in summer. What's more the plants' roots will exhaust the compost in no time. Use pots at least 25cm (10in) in diameter, and preferably more. You'll find them much easier to look after than their smaller relations.

Any container you use *must* have holes in its base. If it hasn't, then in winter it will turn into a reservoir that spells death to plant roots.

Almost every flowering plant you grow will need good light to perform well. If your pots have to be positioned in shade, you'll need to choose your plants very carefully. There are recommendations on page 27.

Elegant containers are all very well, but do make sure that they won't fall over if they are given a gentle nudge. There's nothing more heartbreaking than having your

Plants in pots and hanging baskets adorn this pergola

carefully cherished planting scheme shatter on a concrete patio because it wasn't firmly achored. If the site is exposed to strong winds, rig up some kind of windbreak to protect the plants.

Compost

The kind of compost you use depends on the type of container and the type of plant it will hold. One thing applies right across the board – *never* use garden soil. It's fine for plants in the garden because their roots can explore as far as they wish. Drainage is probably good in the garden, too, thanks to the deep structure of the soil and the cultivations you undertake with spade, fork, rake and hoe. But in a pot, garden soil is disastrous. It drains badly, and it offers plant roots little food in such a restricted area. Any weed seeds or pests and diseases in the soil will quickly swamp the plants so that they have an uphill struggle to grow well.

Which type?   Pay a pound or two for some decent potting compost that comes ready mixed in a sack. There are two basic kinds:

- Loam-based compost such as John Innes
- Peat-based compost such as Levington, Kerimure and Arthur Bowers

For pots and tubs that are to hold large and vigorous plants on a permanent basis – trees and shrubs, for instance – use a loam-based compost. It's heavier, thus increasing stability, and it holds on to its nutrients longer than peat-based compost.

For bedding plants, for window boxes, hanging baskets and for pots on balconies and roof gardens where lightness is important, use a peat-based compost.

The two composts mixed together make a good compromise compost that's well aerated without being too light, and this mixture can be used for any plant in any container.

If rhododendrons and azaleas are your favourite tub-grown plants, give them a mixture of a peat-based compost and John Innes Ericaceous compost, which lacks the lime that rhododendrons and azaleas hate. (They also hate drought, too, so take care that water is never in short supply.)

Drainage

As well as having plenty of holes in the base so that excess water can escape, it's also a good idea if a container has a layer of rough material in its bottom to prevent the holes from becoming clogged with compost.

Gardeners of old would use crocks – pieces of broken clay flowerpot. If you're not clumsy enough to have a plentiful supply of these, there's no reason why a layer of broken bricks or broken plastic flowerpots should not be put in the base of the pot or tub. Coarse gravel will serve the same purpose. Even with peat-based compost where drainage material is said to be unnecessary, I'd still put some in when the container is to remain outdoors all the year round.

Pots

The flowerpot is the most obvious choice of container, and with hundreds of successful years behind it you can be sure of success. The clay or 'terracotta' pots have a rustic charm plus the advantage of weight, for stability, but make sure that any you intend to leave outdoors all

A selection of the many containers available

the year round are frost resistant. After a few months all clay pots become coated either with a white efflorescence or green algae, so they'll need an occasional scrub to keep them smart.

Plastic pots need no such attention, and they don't shatter so readily as clay pots when dropped and they are cheaper to buy. But they'll never look as natural in many folk's eyes, so pay your money and take your choice.

Pots that are 25, 30 and 35cm (10, 12 and 14in) in diameter are best, but once you're past the 30-cm (12-in) mark the prices of clay pots begin to rocket. One final thing; clay pots are porous and they do tend to dry out faster than plastic pots in summer. An important consideration if you're away a lot.

Tubs

There's no container more handsome than a well-coopered tub that was once half a beer barrel. Make sure its hoops are firmly attached, that the inside and outside are painted with a timber preservative such as Cuprinol

Trailing lobelia, petunias and *Helichrysum petiolatum* in a tub

or Bio Woody (not toxic creosote) and there's every chance that it will have a long life. If possible, cut three or four notches in the rim around the base of the tub to allow water to escape from underneath, and if there are insufficient drainage holes in the bottom, drill out some more. If wood won't fit in with your scheme, there are tubs made of fibreglass, plastic and reconstituted stone.

An old wheelbarrow takes on a new lease of life

Novel containers

I've never been able to come to terms with lavatory pans brimful of bedding, but there are plenty of other containers that are original without being sordid.

Chimney pots are exceptionally handsome and easy to pick up from junk shops at a reasonable price. They'll last for years, but remember that they're bottomless. It's best to use them as pot holders – large flowerpots can be snugly fitted into their rims so that only the chimney is visible.

When your favourite wheelbarrow is past its prime, put it out to grass. Park it and fill it with compost and flowers. It will take on a new lease of life, but, again, remember to make some drainage holes in the base.

Strawberry and parsley pots cost an absolute fortune, but if some generous relation can be persuaded to buy you one of these terracotta beauties for your birthday, why should you worry? The plants are inserted through the holes in the side, roots first, as the pot is filled with compost. When they're established the pot will turn into a tower of flowers and fruits and foliage.

Tower pots are cheaper plastic alternatives to the strawberry pot, and the plants do seem to enjoy growing in them. But beware! This type of pot is very top-heavy and will crash to the ground when given the slightest nudge, unless you can wire it to a nearby support.

A barrel is much more stable, and large holes can be drilled in its side to take the strawberry plants. The only problem here is that it takes an enormous amount of compost to fill it up.

Garage owners can use stacked car tyres as containers (they don't look as bad as you'd think), and if utility is more important than beauty, growing bags will produce plenty of vegetables as well as flowers.

Stately home owners will want urns (not necessarily of the Medici variety), but to my eye, no container looks better than an Ali Baba jar of terracotta, whether it's sitting on a patio or nestling among plants at the front of a border. The only snag is the high price.

Window boxes

If your outlook is dreary – a vista of grey buildings and uninspiring traffic – it's easy to brighten it up with a window box, even if you don't own a windowsill. If the sill is there, then the size of your window box is obvious, but below sill-less windows a sturdy trough can be fastened to brackets that are securely attached to the masonry.

Plain painted boxes are best. Those with busy wrought-iron fronts and those that are brightly coloured will only detract from the plants themselves. Plastic troughs in white or muted green will do nicely, and it won't be long before their fronts are masked by trailing plants. Plastic troughs last for ages.

If it is to hold enough compost to keep your plants happy, your window box should be at least 20cm (8in) deep. There's no reason why it shouldn't overlap the sill

A window box must be securely attached to a wall

11

for 2 to 3cm (about 1in) or so, but if you make it slightly smaller than the width of the sill it will be much easier to lift out for replanting. Drainage holes and a layer of drainage material are essential. A couple of blocks of wood placed under the box will allow surplus water to escape.

Wooden window boxes are simple to make from odd bits of timber. The diagram shows how. Treat the box with a timber preservative such as Cuprinol, and don't plant it up until it's completely dry. Brass or galvanised screws will last longer than nails.

The best window boxes are positioned on sunny sills; in shady sites you'll have to rely a good deal on bright foliage plants (see page 26). Whatever the aspect, remember to choose fairly low-growing plants, otherwise your rooms will gradually turn into caves as the plants block out the light.

A simple window box to make

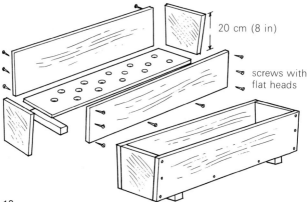

20 cm (8 in)

screws with flat heads

Hanging baskets

Hanging baskets are unsurpassed when it comes to cheering up the air above head height. This is important; miscalculate and you stand a chance of having a permanent headache! There are two basic kinds of basket, one of which isn't a basket at all. The traditional type is a bowl-shaped wire construction, suspended on three chains; the modern type is also bowl shaped, but of solid plastic. It is also fitted with a drip tray which makes it useful where there is frequent pedestrian access around watering time (it saves the unsuspecting passer-by from a soaking). The disadvantage of this type of 'basket' is that nothing can be planted in its sides, so you'll have to rely on the performance of trailers in the top of the basket to mask the lower half.

Wherever your basket is to go, do make sure that it is securely fixed; once full of damp compost and plants it weighs a good deal more than you'd think.

Planting up The plastic type of hanging basket can be planted up quite easily – just like a flowerpot. Wire types need a special technique:

Take the empty basket and sit it on top of a bucket. Persuade your local florist to sell you some sphagnum moss (the green, fluffy stuff that's used as a basis for wreaths). If he won't part with any, cut out a piece of old carpet underlay to act as a basket liner. Snip holes in the underlay at intervals so that plants can be inserted to mask the sides of the basket.

If you've managed to find some moss, spread a 2.5-cm (1-in) layer in the bottom of the basket and sit a saucer (not the best china) on top of it. The saucer helps to retain moisture. Add some compost (peat-based is best because it's lighter than John Innes) and then push several trailing plants through the sides of the basket (roots first, from the outside inwards). Add more moss up the sides of the basket, then more compost and trailers until the basket is full and the sides are evenly planted.

Now you can plant the top. Sit a bushy geranium (pelargonium) or something of a similar shape in the centre, surrounded by smaller plants, like petunias, and edged with trailing lobelia, campanulas or creeping jenny. It's no crime to overplant a hanging basket. I'm all for setting the plants about 10cm (4in) apart so that they rapidly smother the wire and turn the basket into a cheerful orb of leaves and flowers.

Planting up a hanging basket

General care For aerodynamic reasons, hanging baskets are usually planted up for summer displays only. Left out at other times of year they may be badly buffeted by icy blasts that do the plants no good at all. For this reason, plant them up with summer bedding during May and hang them outdoors when all danger of frost is past in early June.

They dry out very quickly. Check them at least once a day – it pays dividends. A basket that dries out just once will often look tatty within a week. Keep the compost moist at all times and you can look forward to a floral extravaganza that may last well into October, with a bit of luck!

If you're lacking in inspiration when it comes to choosing plants for your hanging baskets, see the suggestions on page 27.

Sink gardens

Keen gardeners go green at the sight of an old stone sink or horse trough chock full of alpine and rock plants. There's not much you can do about making a horse trough, without investing in half a ton of concrete, but it's easy to turn an old white porcelain sink into one that looks as near as dash it like stone.

First find your sink. Clean it and throw away the plug. Stand it on two tiers of bricks in its permanent position. Now follow these instructions:

1. Coat the outside of the sink with a bonding agent such as Unibond or Polybond.
2. Mix together your artificial stone coating which consists of 2 parts peat, 1 part sand and 1 part cement.

A sink planted with sedums, saxifrages and other alpines

3. Add water to the mixture to make it moist but not sloppy. It should bind together when squeezed.

4. Pat the mixture on to the outside of the sink to make a 1-cm ($\frac{1}{2}$-in) thick layer *while the bonding agent is still tacky*.

5. Make sure that the mixture is taken just over the inside rim of the sink.

6. Leave the coating to harden for two weeks.

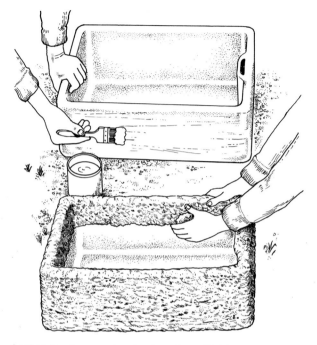

Apply a bonding agent and pat on the artificial stone

You can coarsen the texture of your new 'stone' sink by gently scrubbing the mixture a day or two after it's been patted into place, but take care not to dislodge too much of the coating. Alpine plants like a well-drained, gritty compost, so spread a layer of drainage material in the base of the sink and then fill to within 2.5cm (1in) of the rim with a mixture of 2 parts John Innes No. 1 potting compost and 1 part sharp grit.

Plant the alpines during April and topdress the surface of the compost with a 1- to 2.5-cm ($\frac{1}{2}$ to 1-in) layer of stone chippings. A small rock will make the plants feel at home, and a dwarf conifer such as *Juniperus communis* 'Compressa' will give the planting a lift.

Well cared for it will be years before the trough needs replanting; casualities can be replaced individually as they occur.

Should the frost lift off patches of the stone surface in winter, wait until spring before filling them in with some more of the original mixture.

Planting up and general care

Like any other plants in the garden, those growing in containers do need a bit of attention if they are to do their best. Care starts at planting time.

Thanks to container-grown plants, which are available from nurseries and garden centres all the year round, planting can also be carried out at any time of year except in spells of hard frost or baking drought.

Water any plant quite thoroughly before moving it from its pot into a larger container. Tap it from its pot, sit it on some compost placed over the drainage layer in the new container and firm the new compost around it, disturbing its rootball as little as possible. When planting is completed the compost within the container should rest 2.5 to 5cm (1 to 2in) below the rim to allow for watering. Water every container as soon as planting is complete.

Summer bedding plants should be set out in late May or early June; spring bedding plants and spring-flowering bulbs in September or October.

The backbone of your display can come from evergreen shrubs, deciduous flowering shrubs and even small trees in pots. Perennial border plants grown for their foliage and flowers will also prove reliably long lasting. The annual bedding plants, both for spring and summer, and spring- and summer-flowering bulbs, can be used to add variety to the display as the seasons change.

Climbing plants can be established in tubs close to the walls, and trained over wires or trelliswork attached to the surface. They can also be grown up tripods of canes to bring welcome height to lower plantings.

Vegetables can easily be grown in pots and tubs, just as they can in growing bags, and dwarf fruit trees will do well in large pots or tubs provided they are kept well fed.

Climbing plants should be trained up wire mesh or trellis

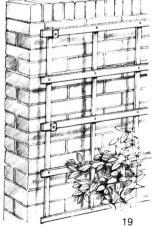

Potted vegetables

Don't make the mistake of thinking that fruits and vegetables are strictly for the kitchen garden. They're not. As well as being tasty many vegetables are really quite good to look at, providing the flower-pot gardener with welcome fresh produce.

I'm not suggesting that you devote your entire patio to grow-bags packed with Brussels sprouts and celery; choose those vegetables that are either totally absent from the shops: things like Swiss chard with its super white-stalked, shiny green leaves; and American or land cress – the next best thing to water cress if you lack a stream – or crops which are especially delectable when harvested fresh: French beans, courgettes and tomatoes.

A dwarf bush tomato looks good in a large terracotta pot

Lettuce, courgettes and peppers in grow bags on a balcony

Grow-bags are not the only containers for vegetables; they'll thrive equally well in a tub, a large flower pot or even a classical urn. The thing to do is to make sure that they have a plentiful supply of nourishing compost, and that the compost is replaced or replenished when each new crop is planted.

You can cheat a bit if you like. Compost that has grown greedy blighters such as tomatoes, peppers and aubergines, will happily feed a few lettuces or radishes the following season, but it would be unfair to expect it to rear another crop of gluttons.

If you're after good-looking vegetables that will add to appearances as well as to your plate, try these:

- Parsley – a good edger anywhere
- 'Salad Bowl' lettuce – frilly and non-hearting
- Leeks – a handsome clump of blue-grey swords!
- Swiss and ruby chard – white stalks on the first, red stalks on the second; both have shiny green leaves
- Red cabbage – superb specimens for urns!
- Beetroot – dark red leaf stalks and red-veined leaves.

Potted fruits

There's nothing to stop you growing gooseberries, red and white currants, peaches and nectarines in pots, though the last-named pair will need a warm and sheltered patio to do well. The secret is to give each of them a pot that holds plenty of compost. Look for a container that's at least 30cm (12in) in diameter and, as the plants grow larger, they'll appreciate the roomier confines of a tub.

How about an apple tree? It's not impossible. Ask at your nursery for a bush tree grafted on to a dwarfing rootstock and it will crop quite happily after a year or two in a large pot or tub of John Innes potting compost No.3. You'll have to feed the tree regularly in summer and prune it each year in winter – shortening the shoots by about a third, but you'll still be able to enjoy a tasty, if somewhat reduced, harvest. Rootstocks have complicated-sounding code-names. Pick the wrong one and your tree will grow into a giant. The number to remember for pot-grown trees is M 27, but failing that go for M 9. It's a rootstock that keeps them well in check, but still allows them to grow to around head height.

Container care

Watering really is the secret of success with plants in pots. Drought is their bitterest enemy, and it pays to check every container every day in summer. In winter waterlogging can be a nuisance. If your site seems to receive more than its fair share of water, wrap a canopy of polythene over the surface of each container to deflect unwanted soakings.

Plants that are permanent residents in pots should be perked up each spring with a topdressing. Scrape away the top 5cm (2in) of compost and replace it with fresh. Alternatively give the plant a larger pot and more fresh compost. It's up to you to decide just how big you want your potted plants to grow. The larger the pot, the more generous will be their growth. Keep them in too small a pot for too long a time and they will become sickly as well as stunted, so use your judgement to decide when a plant needs splitting up, planting out in the garden or just moving into a larger pot.

Plants need food as well as water. Between April and September they'll appreciate a dose of diluted liquid fertiliser once a month. General fertiliser will do for foliage plants. Flowering plants will benefit from tomato fertiliser which promotes both flowering and fruiting.

Plants that are growing tall and spindly generally need more light, but they can also be pinched back to encourage bushiness. Nip out their shoot tips quite low down and the sideshoots will sprout to improve the overall shape.

Remember to remove any weeds that grow in the containers, and to treat pests and diseases quickly before they spread to other plants. Weeds can be discouraged in

Petunias are ideal plants for containers or hanging baskets

Pelargoniums, creeping jenny and petunias in a window box

larger containers with a layer of washed pea shingle or even smooth pebbles – these show off foliage plants a treat.

Seasonal changes

If your window boxes and tubs are stripped of their occupants and replanted twice a year (for spring and summer displays), do make sure that the compost is replenished. Fill the container with fresh compost for the summer bedding and then it can simply be topped up when the spring bedders are put in. Remove and replace it completely for the summer bedding the following year. In this way, one lot of compost will support two displays. Your show may suffer if you try to make it do more.

The plants

You can plant anything in a container provided you realise that it may have a limited life when growing in such a restricted space. This isn't the case with bedding plants, or with many small or low-growing plants, but it is true of trees and shrubs.

However, that shouldn't stop you from being original in your choice of plants. A bit of inspiration never did anybody any harm, so here are some suggestions of plants that are especially suited to being grown in pots and tubs, window boxes and hanging baskets to give a good show all the year round.

Plants for window boxes

Spring show (September planting): dwarf double daisies, forget-me-nots, pansies, crocuses, muscari, dwarf irises (reticulata cultivars), short-stemmed tulips (Greigii and Kaufmanniana cultivars), dwarf narcissi (such as 'W.P. Milner', 'Little Witch', 'Tete-a-tete') hyacinths, aubrieta, wallflowers (short-growing cultivars), polyanthus.

Summer show (late May planting): ageratum, alyssum, antirrhinum (snapdragon), aster, *Begonia semperflorens*, tuberous begonias, celosia, fuchsias, gazania, golden creeping jenny (lysimachia), mesembryanthemum, nemesia, petunia, French marigolds, tagetes, thyme, verbena.

Permanent residents: dwarf box, ivies, heathers (especially winter flowering), blue fescue grass (*Festuca glauca*), *Juniperus communis* 'Compressa' (as a central highlight), mossy saxifrages, *Hebe pinguifolia* 'Pagei'.

Herbs such as thyme, sage, parsley (renew every other year), chives, marjoram, winter savoury, basil (renew every year).

Plants for hanging baskets

In the top: pelargoniums (geraniums), petunias, verbena, ageratum, alyssum, begonias (both semperflorens and pendulous types), fuchsias, dusty miller (*Senecio cineraria*).

On the sides: trailing lobelia, ivy-leaved pelargoniums, golden creeping jenny (lysimachia), ivies, nasturtiums (tropaeolum).

Plants for shade

Maidenhair fern (adiantum), foxglove, arabis, astrantia, camellia, bamboo (arundinaria), asplenium, box (buxus), bishop's hat (epimedium), euphorbia, false castor oil (fatsia), cranesbills (true geraniums), ivies, hostas, heuchera, liriope, periwinkle (vinca), mahonia, pieris, rhododendrons, viburnums.

Architectural pot plants

Mahonia, cordyline, yucca, tree of heaven* (ailanthus), dawn redwood* (metasequoia), false castor oil (fatsia), hostas, ferns, New Zealand flax (phormium), Japanese maples (*Acer palmatum* and cultivars), junipers, ornamental cabbages, golden false acacia (*Robinia pseudoacacia* 'Frisia'), smoke bush (*Cotinus coggygria* 'Royal Purple'), sumach (*Rhus typhina*).

---

* These will eventually grow to form sizable trees; their life in a container should be limited to around five years.

Shrubs and bamboos in containers create a cool leafy haven

Mixed bulbs and violas make a cheery spring planting

Winter colour

Either for their flowers or foliage, these plants are worth growing in containers to bring brightness during the dreariest months of the year.

November Liriope, Algerian iris (*Iris unguicularis*), true autumn-flowering crocuses such as *Crocus longiflorus*, *C. medius* and *C. cancellatus*, heaths (*Erica carnea* and *E.* × *darleyensis* cultivars), laurustinus (*Viburnum tinus*), false castor oil (fatsia), *Hebe* 'Autumn Glory', *Viburnum fragrans*, autumn cherry (*Prunus subhirtella* 'Autumnalis'), winter jasmine (*Jasminum nudiflorum*).

December Algerian iris (*Iris unguicularis*), true autumn crocuses such as *Crocus laevigatus*, *C. imperati*, snowdrops (galanthus), heaths (*Erica carnea* and *E.* × *darleyensis* cultivars), witch hazel (*Hamamelis mollis*), *Elaeagnus pungens* 'Maculata', variegated hollies, winter jasmine (*Jasminum nudiflorum*), winter honeysuckle (*Lonicera fragrantissima*), *Viburnum fragrans*.

January Christmas roses (*Helleborus niger*), Lenten rose (*Helleborus orientalis*), stinking hellebore (*Helleborus foetidus*), lungworts (pulmonaria), more snowdrops, dwarf irises (*Iris reticulata*), heaths (*Erica carnea* and *E.* × *darleyensis* cultivars), *Garrya elliptica*, mahonias, sarcococcas, *Viburnum* × *bodnantense*, winter jasmine (*Jasminum nudiflorum*).

February Spotted laurel (aucuba), bergenias, hellebores as for January (plus other species), lungworts (pulmonaria), more winter-flowering crocuses such as *Crocus chrysanthus*, *C. biflorus* and *C. etruscus*, dog's tooth violets (erythronium), more snowdrops, winter-flowering irises, *Anemone blanda*, kabschia saxifrages, camellias, heaths (as January), mahonias, *Pieris japonica*,

Rhododendron 'Christmas Cheer', japonica (chaenomeles), Harry Lauder's walking stick (*Corylus avellana* 'Contorta').

March   Bergenias, more hellebores, lungworts (pulmonaria), primroses, chionodoxa, crocuses, more snowdrops, narcissi, early tulips, *Anemone blanda*, drumstick primulas (*Primula denticulata*), kabschia saxifrages, camellias, heaths (as February), *Pieris floribunda*, *Pieris japonica*, japonica (chaenomeles), mezereon (*Daphne mezereum*), *Magnolia stellata*, forsythia, *Prunus triloba*.

A few of these in pots are bound to brighten anybody's winter!

Witch hazel, *Hamamelis mollis*, (left) and dog's tooth violet, *Erythronium dens-canis* (below)

Index